DE 16 02

Sp juv 611.98 KLI
Amoroso, Cynthia
Feet = Pies
mada

WITHDRAWN

DAMAGES NOTED 5-11-16
Stains inside front covers. J on

Let's Read About Our Bodies
Conozcamos nuestro cuerpo

Feet/Pies

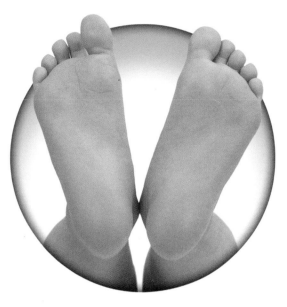

Cynthia Klingel & Robert B. Noyed
photographs by/fotografías por Gregg Andersen

Reading consultant/Consultora de lectura: Cecilia Minden-Cupp, Ph.D.,
Adjunct Professor, College of Continuing and Professional Studies, University of Virginia

WeeklyReader.
EARLY LEARNING LIBRARY

For a free color catalog describing Weekly Reader® Early Learning Library's list of high-quality books, call 1-800-542-2595 or fax your request to (414) 332-3567.

Library of Congress Cataloging-in-Publication Data

Klingel, Cynthia.
    Feet = Pies / by Cynthia Klingel and Robert B. Noyed. — [Bilingual ed.]
      p. cm. — (Let's read about our bodies = Conozcamos nuestro cuerpo)
    Includes bibliographical references and index.
    Summary: A bilingual introduction to feet, what they are used for, and how to take care of them.
    ISBN 0-8368-3073-3 (lib. bdg.)
    1. Foot—Juvenile literature. [1. Foot. 2. Spanish language materials—Bilingual.] I. Title: Pies.
II. Noyed, Robert B. III. Title.
QM549.K54   2002
611'.98—dc21   2001055091

This edition first published in 2002 by
Weekly Reader® Early Learning Library
330 West Olive Street, Suite 100
Milwaukee, WI 53212 USA

Copyright © 2002 by Weekly Reader® Early Learning Library

An Editorial Directions book
Editors: E. Russell Primm and Emily Dolbear
Translators: Tatiana Acosta and Guillermo Gutiérrez
Art direction, design, and page production: The Design Lab
Photographer: Gregg Andersen
Weekly Reader® Early Learning Library art direction: Tammy Gruenewald
Weekly Reader® Early Learning Library page layout: Katherine A. Goedheer

Printed in the United States of America

1 2 3 4 5 6 7 8 9 06 05 04 03 02

Note to Educators and Parents

As a Reading Specialist I know that books for young children should engage their interest, impart useful information, and motivate them to want to learn more.

Let's Read About Our Bodies is a new series of books designed to help children understand the value of good health and of taking care of their bodies.

A young child's active mind is engaged by the carefully chosen subjects. The imaginative text works to build young vocabularies. The short, repetitive sentences help children stay focused as they develop their own relationship with reading. The bright, colorful photographs of children enjoying good health habits complement the text with their simplicity to both entertain and encourage young children to want to learn — and read — more.

These books are designed to be used by adults as "read-to" books to share with children to encourage early literacy in the home, school, and library. They are also suitable for more advanced young readers to enjoy on their own.

Una nota a los educadores y a los padres

Como especialista en lectura, sé que los libros infantiles deben interesar a los niños, proporcionar información útil y motivarlos a aprender.

Conozcamos nuestro cuerpo es una nueva serie de libros pensada para ayudar a los niños a entender la importancia de la salud y del cuidado del cuerpo.

Los temas, cuidadosamente seleccionados, mantienen ocupada la activa mente del niño. El texto, lleno de imaginación, facilita el enriquecimiento del vocabulario infantil. Las oraciones, breves y repetitivas, ayudan a los niños a centrarse en la actividad mientras desarrollan su propia relación con la lectura. Las bellas fotografías de niños que disfrutan de buenos hábitos de salud complementan el texto con su sencillez, y consiguen entretener a los niños y animarlos a aprender nuevos conceptos y a leer más.

Estos libros están pensados para que los adultos se los lean a los niños, con el fin de fomentar la lectura incipiente en el hogar, en la escuela y en la biblioteca. También son adecuados para que los jóvenes lectores más avanzados los disfruten leyéndolos por su cuenta.

Cecilia Minden-Cupp, Ph.D., Adjunct Professor,
College of Continuing and Professional Studies, University of Virginia

These are my feet!

¡Éstos son mis pies!

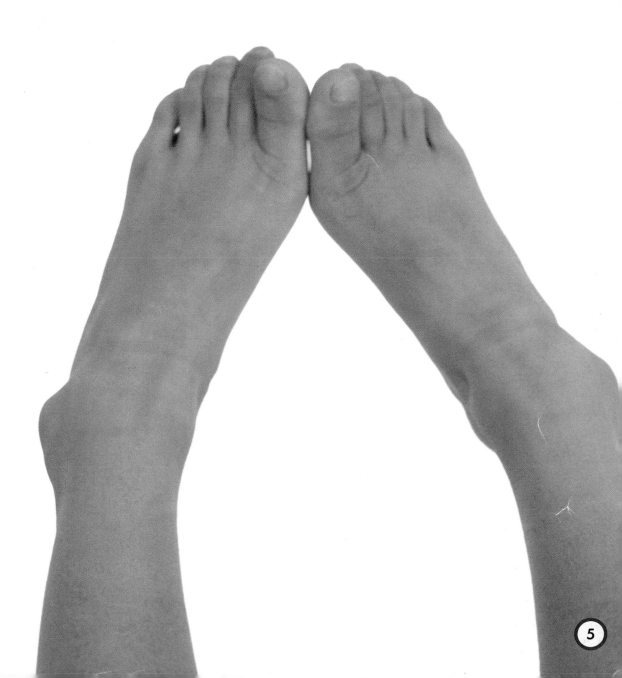

I have two feet.

- - - - - - -

Tengo dos pies.

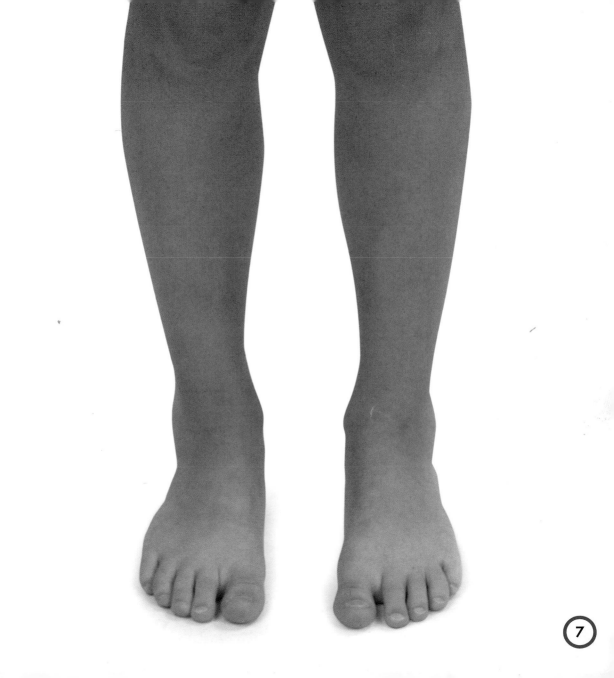

⑦

My feet are small.
Some feet are big.

- - - - - - -

Mis pies son pequeños.
Algunos pies son grandes.

My feet help me
walk and run.

- - - - - - -

Los pies me ayudan
a caminar y a correr.

I have ten toes.
I can wiggle my toes.
Can you?

Tengo diez dedos en
los pies. Puedo agitar
los deditos. ¿Puedes
hacerlo tú?

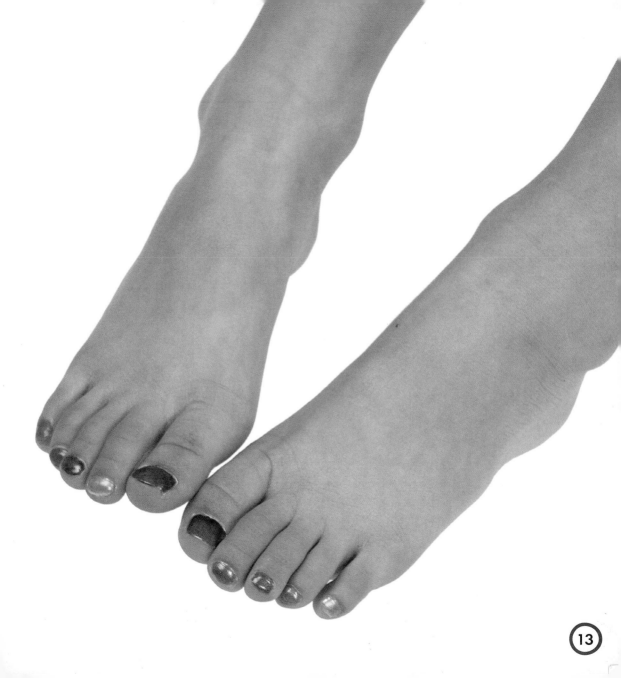

I keep my toenails short and clean.

Mantengo mis uñas cortas y limpias.

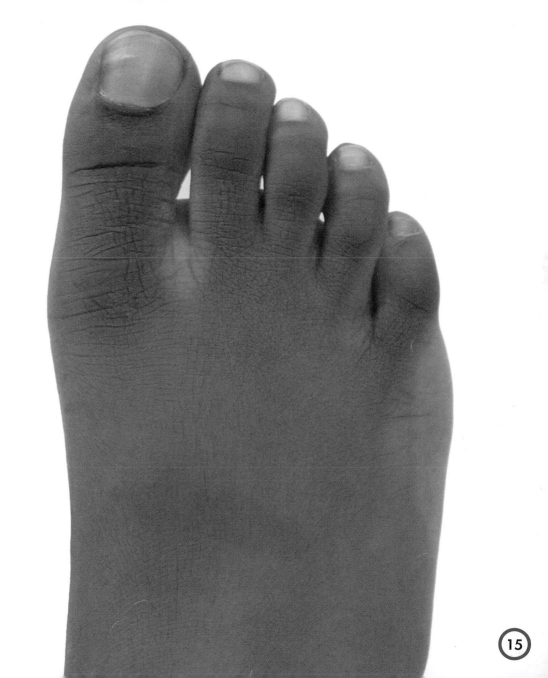

I keep my feet warm.
I wear socks.

- - - - - - -

Mantengo mis pies
calientes. Llevo medias.

I keep my feet safe.
I wear shoes.

- - - - - - -

Me cuido los pies.
Llevo zapatos.

Feet are fun to tickle!

¡Es divertido hacer cosquillas en los pies!

Glossary/Glosario

tickle—to touch the body in a way that causes a tingling feeling

hacer cosquillas—tocar una parte del cuerpo de manera que produce un hormigueo

toenails—a thin, hard layer of material growing at the end of each toe

uñas de los pies— capa delgada y dura que crece al final de cada dedo

wiggle—to move from side to side in short, sudden movements

agitar—mover de un lado a otro en movimientos rápidos

For More Information/Más información

Fiction Books/Libros de ficción

Hamm, Diane Johnson. *How Many Feet in the Bed?* New York: Simon and Schuster, 1991.

Paul, Ann Whitford. *Hello Toes! Hello Feet!* New York: DK Publishing, 2000.

Rau, Dana Meachen. *Feet.* Danbury, Conn.: Children's Press, 2000.

Nonfiction Books/Libros de no ficción

Cromwell, Sharon. *Why Do My Feet Fall Asleep?* Chicago: Heinemann Library, 1998.

Swanson, Diane. *Up Close: Feet That Suck and Feed.* New York: Greystone Books, 2000.

Yagyu, Genichiro. *The Soles of Your Feet.* New York: Kane/Miller Books, 1997.

Web Sites/Páginas Web
Why Does My Foot Fall Asleep?
kidshealth.org/kid/talk/qa/foot_asleep.html
For information about sleepy feet

Index/Índice

About the Authors/Información sobre los autores

Cynthia Klingel has worked as a high school English teacher and an elementary school teacher. She is currently the curriculum director for a Minnesota school district. Cynthia Klingel lives with her family in Mankato, Minnesota.

Cynthia Klingel ha trabajado como maestra de inglés de secundaria y como maestra de primaria. Actualmente es la directora de planes de estudio de un distrito escolar de Minnesota. Cynthia Klingel vive con su familia en Mankato, Minnesota.

Robert B. Noyed started his career as a newspaper reporter. Since then, he has worked in school communications and public relations at the state and national level. Robert B. Noyed lives with his family in Brooklyn Center, Minnesota.

Robert B. Noyed comenzó su carrera como reportero en un periódico. Desde entonces ha trabajado en comunicación escolar y relaciones públicas a nivel estatal y nacional. Robert B. Noyed vive con su familia en Brooklyn Center, Minnesota.